Vocabulary chart

Title	Vocabulary	Sounds	Bookband Level
Magic Tricks	as, be, black, but, by, called, do, down, good, help, her, how, make, man, not, now, out, pull, off, one, put, so, some, than, that, three, two, water, what, will, with, your	'ai' (air, tablespoon, make, say) 'oo' (spoon, loose)	6 orange
Houses Then and Now	an, by, called, did, had, has, have, here, house, new, not, now, old, one, out, people, put, then, there, three, two, water, were, with	'oo' (room, cool, food) 'oa' (board) 'ee' (heating)	7 turquoise
E-mails Home	again, another, but, do, down, from, had, has, have, home, made, many, new, next, now, one, out, people, saw, so, some, there, time, very, water, were, when, where, your; and colour words, black, red, orange	'ai' (shape, made, safe) 'ee' (keep)	6 orange
Looking after your Dog	after, be, do, down, from, good, here, if, little, make, may, new, off, one, out, over, put, so, some, take, that, them, there, two, water, what, when, where, will, with, your	'ee' (feed, cleaned, lead) 'oo' (food, shampoo)	7 turquoise
Public Art	an, ball, be, by, called, could, four, from, has, have, live, made, make, not, or, out, people, some, that, them, then, there, these, time, tree, very, water, were, where, with	'ie' (bright) 'ai' (made, make)	7 turquoise
Wonders of the World	an, back, be, but, by, called, five, good, has, little, live, made, more, much, not, one, or, over, so, some, them, then, that, there, three, very, water, when, where, with, would	'ie' (highest) 'ee' (reef, Greenland)	9 gold

Teaching objectives

	Teacher's Notes			Guided Reading Cards
	Speaking and listening	Reading	Writing	Reading
Magic Tricks				
Scotland	Listening/Talking Level A	Level A	Level A	Level A
N. Ireland	Activities a, c, f Outcomes a, b, c, d, e	Activities a, b Outcomes c, e, f, i	Opportunities a Outcomes a, b, c, d	Activities a, b Outcomes c, e, f, i Writing Outcomes b, d
Wales	Oracy Range 1, 3, 5 Skills 1, 2, 3	Range 1, 4, 7 Skills 3, 4, 5	Range 1, 2, 3 Skills 4, 5, 6	Range 1, 2, 3 Skills 1, 2, 3 Writing Skills 5, 6
NC/NLS Y1T3	1c 1d 1f 2d 4a	T2 T19 S3 S7 W1 W2	T20	T19 T21 S6 W1
Houses Then and Now				
Scotland	Listening/Talking Level A	Level A	Level A	Level A
N. Ireland	Activities a, f Outcomes a, b, c, d, e	Activities a, b Outcomes e, f, i	Opportunities a Outcomes b, d	Activities a, b Outcomes e, f, i Writing Outcomes b, d
Wales	Oracy Range 1, 3 Skills 3, 4, 5	Range 1, 2, 3 Skills 1, 2, 3	Range 3, 4, 7 Skills 5, 6	Range 1, 2, 3 Skills 1, 2, 3 Writing Skills 5, 6
NC/NLS Y1T3	1d 2d 3a 3e	T17 T19 S1 S2 W4 W6	T21	T17 T19 T21 S3 W6
Emails Home				
Scotland	Listening/Talking Level A	Level A	Level A	Level A
N. Ireland	Activities a, f Outcomes b, c, d, e	Activities a, b Outcomes b, e, f, i	Outcomes b, e, f, i Outcomes b, d	Activities a, b Outcomes b, e, f, i Writing Outcomes b, d
Wales	Oracy Range 1, 3 Skills 3, 4, 5	Range 1, 2, 3 Skills 1, 2, 3	Range 3, 4, 7 Skills 5, 6	Range 1, 2, 3 Skills 1, 2, 3 Writing Skills 5, 6
NC/NLS Y1T3	1c 1d 2d 3a	T17 T19 S2 S4 W2 W6	T20	T2 T20 S3 W1
Looking after your Dog				
Scotland	Listening/Talking Level A	Level A	Level A	Level A
N. Ireland	Activities a, f Outcomes b, c, d, e	Activities a, b Outcomes c, f, i	Opportunities a Outcomes b, d	Activities a, b Outcomes c, f, i Writing Outcomes b, d
Wales	Oracy Range 1, 3 Skills 3, 4, 5	Range 1, 2, 3 Skills 1, 2, 3	Range 3, 4, 7 Skills 5, 6	Range 1, 2, 3 Skills 1, 2, 3 Writing Skills 5, 6
NC/NLS Y1T3	1d 2d 3a 3e	T2 T19 S3 S4 W1 W2	T21	T2 T22 S7 W1 W6

ireflies
tage 5

ill Howell

Teaching Notes

Contents

Introduction

Fireflies is an exciting non-fiction series within *Oxford Reading Tree*. The books are specially designed to be used alongside the Stage 1 stories. They provide practice of reading skills in a non-fiction context whilst using the same simple, repetitive sentences as the *Oxford Reading Tree* stories. They also contain a selection of high frequency vocabulary. Each stage builds on the reading skills and vocabulary from previous stages, and helps children to read with growing confidence. As children read these books, they should be encouraged to read independently through: using their knowledge of letter sounds; learning to recognize high frequency words on sight; using the pictures and the sense of the story to work out new vocabulary.

To help children approach each new book in this stage with confidence, prepare the children for reading by talking about the book, asking questions and using these Teacher's Notes and the additional *Guided Reading Cards* and *Take-Home Cards*.

How to introduce the books

Before reading the book, always read the title and talk about the picture on the cover. Go through the book together, looking at the pictures and talking about them. If there are words that are new or unfamiliar, point them out and read them with the children.

This booklet provides suggestions for using the books with groups of children or individuals. You can use the ideas with shared, group or guided reading sessions, or with individual children. Suggestions are also provided for writing, speaking and listening and cross-curricular links. You can use these suggestions to follow on from your reading, or use at another time.

Guided Reading Cards are available for each book. These provide more detailed guidance for using the books for guided reading. *Take-Home Cards* are also available for each book. These provide prompts and suggestions for parents reading with their children. You can store the relevant card with each book in your "Take-Home" selection of titles.

Public Art				
Scotland	Listening/Talking Level A	Level A	Level A	Level A
N. Ireland	Activities a, f Outcomes b, c, d, e	Activities a, b Outcomes b, e, f, k	Opportunities a Outcomes b, d	Activities a, b Outcomes b, e, f, k Writing Outcomes b, d
Wales	Oracy Range 1, 3 Skills 3, 4, 5	Range 1, 2, 3 Skills 1, 2	Range 3, 4, 7 Skills 5, 6	Range 1, 2, 3 Skills 1, 2 Writing Skills 5, 6
NC/NLS Y1T3	1d 2d 3a 3e	T2 T4 S2 S5 W2 W6	T22	T19 T22 S5 W6
Wonders of the World				
Scotland	Listening/Talking Level A	Level A	Level A	Level A
N. Ireland	Activities a, f Outcomes b, c, d, e	Activities a, b Outcomes e, f, i	Opportunities a Outcomes b, d	Activities a, b Outcomes e, f, i Writing Outcomes b, d
Wales	Oracy Range 1, 3 Skills 3, 4, 5	Range 1, 2, 3 Skills 1, 2	Range 3, 4, 7 Skills 5, 6	Range 1, 2, 3 Skills 1, 2 Writing Skills 5, 6
NC/NLS Y1T3	1d 2d 3a 3e	T17 T18 S3 S4 W1 W7	T22	T19 T21 S4 W5

Magic Tricks

Reading the book with individuals or guided reading groups

NB for additional and more detailed guidance on guided reading see Stage 5 Guided Reading Cards (available separately, ISBN 0 19 919770 9). Take-Home Cards are also available, providing guidance for parents/carers (ISBN 0 19 919769 5).

Introducing the book

- Look at the front cover. Ask the children what type of book this is going to be?
- Read the title together, and ask the children to predict what sort of information will be in the book.
- Ask them to read the back cover blurb to confirm their ideas.
- Look together through the book and point out any words the children may have difficulty with e.g. thumb, mirror.

During reading

- Encourage the children to read the book. Praise the children for taking notice of the punctuation and using it to give expression to their reading.
- Prompt the children to use the initial sounds to work out the new and unfamiliar words, and to predict words that fit.

Observing Check that the children:

- use a variety of strategies to work out new words (T2)
- use expression appropriate to exclamation marks (S3)
- read the high frequency words on sight (W2)

After reading

- Ask the children:
  How many magic tricks did you learn about?
  What would you use the index for in this book?

Group and independent reading activities

Text level work

Objectives   To identify simple questions and use text to find answers
To locate parts of text that give particular information (T19)

- Ask the children to work with a partner. Tell them to read the text to themselves, and to ask questions about what they are reading to their partner, e.g. Which trick needs a tablespoon?
- Ask their partners to find the pages in the text where the answer is to be found.

Sentence level work

Objective   To add question marks to questions (S7)

Prepare:
the sentences below written on a board, a computer or on paper with missing punctuation:
Put your fingers together
How do you pick up the spoon
Who will help you
Where do you put the sugar cube

- Ask the children to rewrite the sentences and add the correct punctuation. Early finishers can find the answers to the questions in the text.

Word level work

Objective   The common spelling patterns for the long vowel phoneme "ee'" (W1)

- Read page 6 to the children and ask them to notice how the "ee" sound in "need" is spelt.
- Discuss how the long "ee" sound can be spelt, and ask the children to suggest other words with this sound.
- Ask the children to look through the text and collect as many different ways of spelling the "ee" sound as they can find. Ways they may find include "ie" as in "piece", "e" as in "before", "ee" as in "squeeze", "ea" as in "leave".

Speaking and listening activities for groups

Objectives 1c) organize what they say; 1d) focus on the main point; 1f) take into account the needs of their listeners; 2d) listen to others' reactions; 4a) use language and actions to explore and convey situations and characters

You will need:
some props to enable the children to try out the magic tricks

- Ask some of the children to practise one of the tricks, and to perform it for the rest of the class.
- Some children may be able to show other tricks that they know.
- Discuss what a magician needs to do to trick the audience.

Cross-curricular links
◀▶ ICT (QCA 1F)
Understanding instructions and making things happen

Writing

Objective To write simple recounts linked to topics of interest (T20)

- Read page 6 of "The Spoon" trick with the children.
- Ask the children to imagine they have done the trick and are writing about what they did. Ask them to say how the sentences would have to be changed to show what happened in the past, i.e. using the personal pronoun "I" and past tense verbs.
- Ask them to write the remaining stages of the trick as if describing what they did.

Houses Then and Now

Reading the book with individuals or guided reading groups

NB for additional and more detailed guidance on guided reading see Stage 5 Guided Reading Cards (available separately, ISBN 0 19 919770 9). Take-Home Cards are also available, providing guidance for parents/carers (ISBN 0 19 919769 5).

Introducing the book

- Look at the front cover. Ask the children what sort of book this is. Encourage them to give a reason for their ideas, e.g. there are photographs on the cover.
- Ask the children to read the title. Read the back cover blurb together, and ask them if they think their ideas about the book were correct.
- Look through the book to confirm their ideas, and point out any words that might be unfamiliar to them, e.g. "parlour", "mangle".

During reading

- Encourage the children to read the book. As you listen, encourage the children to talk about what is happening in the pictures.
- Prompt the children to use the picture clues and initial sound to work out the new and unfamiliar words.
- Ask the children to talk about the comparison chart on pages 22–23.

Observing Check that the children:

- ▪ recognize that the chart on pages 22–23 gives the same information but in another form (T17)
- ▪ use the grammar of a sentence to help them work out new words (S2)
- ▪ read high frequency words on sight (W4)

After reading

- Ask the children:
  What does this book tell us about?
  How do the pictures help us understand the information?

Group and independent reading activities

Text level work

Objective To identify simple questions and use text to find answers (T19)

You will need:
the following word cards:
What? Where? When? Why?

- Ask the children to work in small groups. Tell them to take turns to pick a question card, and use it to make up a question for the rest of the group about houses then and now.
- Ask the group to find the page in the text that gives the answer.

Sentence level work

Objective To expect reading to make sense and check if it does not (S1)

Prepare:
the sentences below written on a board, a computer or on pieces of paper with missing words written separately alongside them:
This was built in 1903. house
One of the is called the parlour. rooms
This house has a of rooms. lot
Each bathroom has taps with hot and water. cold
The clothes were washed by in the washing tub. hand

- Ask the children to read the sentences and work out where the last word on each line should go to make the sentences right.
- Encourage them to use the book, if necessary. Praise the children who re-read the sentence to check if it makes sense.

Word level work

Objective To investigate and learn spellings of verbs with "ed" (past tense) endings (W6)

- Read page 7 to the children and discuss how to turn the verbs "watch" and "listen" into past tense verbs.
- Ask the children to look through the text and find other verbs that can have an "ed" ending.
- Some children could add other verbs from their own experience.

Speaking and listening activities for groups

Objectives 1d) focus on the main point; 2d) listen to others' reactions; 3a) take turns in speaking; 3e) give reasons for opinions

You will need:
pictures of homes from different periods and cultures

- Allow the children time to look at the pictures.
- Encourage them to compare the different sorts of homes and their settings.
- Ask the children:
  Can you see anything that is the same in the pictures?
  Who do you think lives in these houses?
  Which house would you like to live in?

Cross-curricular links
◀▶ **Art (QCA 2C)**
Explore shape and pattern in buildings
History (QCA 2)
Explore similarities and differences in homes of today and of the past
ICT (QCA 1D)
Labelling and classifying – use personal descriptions to describe objects

Writing

Objective To use the language and features of non-fiction texts, e.g. labelled diagrams (T21)

- Ask the children to read the information in the chart on pages 22–23.
- Discuss the items pictured in the "Now" column with the children. Ask them to say which of the "Now" list they have in their own houses, and suggest others that could go on the list.
- Tell them to draw items for their own "Now" list, and to label the items to show what they are.
- Provide a word bank or dictionary for children who need it.

E-mails Home

Reading the book with individuals or guided reading groups

NB for additional and more detailed guidance on guided reading see Stage 5 Guided Reading Cards (available separately, ISBN 0 19 919770 9). Take-Home Cards are also available, providing guidance for parents/carers (ISBN 0 19 919769 5).

Introducing the book

- Look at the front cover. Ask the children what type of book this is going to be? Encourage them to look for clues in the cover illustration.
- Ask the children to read the title and the back cover blurb, and predict what the book will be about.
- Look through the book to confirm the children's ideas.
- Discuss what e-mails are and how they are written.

During reading

- Encourage the children to read the book. Praise the children who read the repeated sentences fluently.
- Prompt the children to use their knowledge of sounds, and to break words into syllables to help them with unfamiliar words, e.g. "Kalahari".

Observing Check that the children:

- understand that the e-mails contain factual information (T17)
- predict words from the grammar of sentences (S2)
- read the high frequency words on sight (W2)

After reading

- Ask the children:
  What is happening in this book?
  Who do you think the e-mails are being sent to?

Group and independent reading activities

Text level work

Objective To identify simple questions and use text to find answers (T19)

- Ask the children to work with a partner. Ask the children to choose one of the places featured in the text, to read the relevant pages, and to think of a question about it to ask their partner.
- Tell them to use the index to find the page with the answer and read it to their partner.

Sentence level work

Objective About word order, e.g. re-ordering sentences (S4)

Prepare:
the following sentences written on strips of paper:
Thanks for your email.
I am having a great trip.
This morning I went for a walk.
Do you know where I was?

- Ask the children to work with a partner. Tell them to choose a sentence and to cut it into individual words, and swap them with their partner.
- Tell them to arrange the new sentence into a word order that makes sense, and to check it with the text.

Word level work

Objective To investigate and learn spellings of verbs with "ed" (past tense), "ing" (present tense) endings (W6)

- Read the text on page 3 with the children.
- Ask the children to say what the person who sent the e-mail did, i.e. "went for a walk".
- Write "I walk" on the board. Ask the children to suggest what is needed to change this into something that has already happened, i.e. "I walked".
- Discuss how to change it into something that is still happening, i.e. "I am walking".
- Ask the children to suggest other verbs that can be used in these two ways and draw up a list from the children's suggestions for future use.

Speaking and listening activities for groups

Objectives 1c) organize what they say; 1d) focus on the main point; 2d) listen to others' reactions; 3a) take turns in speaking

You will need:
atlases or a globe

- Discuss the places in the text and look at the maps in the book. Together identify where the places in the book are on a map or globe. Talk about the distance that is covered from the first e-mail message to the last one. Ask the children to say why the author of the messages used e-mail. Ask the children what other ways there are to send messages home.
- Ask each child to say who they would send a message to if they were on holiday, and what they would say.

Cross-curricular links
◀▶ **Geography (QCA 5)**
Where in the world is Barnaby Bear? If possible, encourage parents and friends to send e-mails to the school from different locations.
Geography (QCA 24)
Passport to the world

Writing

Objective To write simple recounts linked to topics of interest (T20)

- Discuss with the children what the author of the e-mails did in the text. Scribe some of their suggestions – using the 3rd person, e.g. He went for a walk. He saw a big building.
- Ask the children to choose one of the locations, and to rewrite the e-mail as a 3rd person recount.

Looking after your Dog

Reading the book with individuals or guided reading groups

NB for additional and more detailed guidance on guided reading see Stage 5 Guided Reading Cards (available separately, ISBN 0 19 919770 9). Take-Home Cards are also available, providing guidance for parents/carers (ISBN 0 19 919769 5).

Introducing the book

- Look at the front cover. Ask the children what type of book this is going to be? Will it tell a story or give information?
- Ask the children to read the title and the back cover blurb.
- Ask them if any of them have a pet dog, and do they think this book would help them.
- Look at the contents page and talk about the list.

During reading

- Encourage the children to read the book. Encourage the children to read on to get the sense of a paragraph, and to re-read it to check any new or difficult words.
- Praise children for recognizing punctuation and using it to help them read with pace and expression.

Observing Check that the children:

- use a variety of strategies to make sense of their reading (T2)
- read aloud with pace and expression appropriate to the grammar, e.g. pausing at full stops (S3)
- read high frequency words confidently (W2)

After reading

- Ask the children to read the index on page 24.
- Ask: *What sort of information does this book give us? Can you find the pages that tell you how to wash your dog?*

Group and independent reading activities

Text level work

Objective To identify simple questions and use text to find answers
To locate parts of text that give particular information (T19)

- Ask the children to read the contents page, and to think of two things they would like to know for each heading.
- Ask the children to write down their questions on separate pieces of paper.
- Collect all the questions, and tell the children to pick one out, and use the contents and index to find the answers.

Sentence level work

Objective To learn about word order, e.g. by re-ordering sentences, predicting words from previous text (S4)

Prepare:
the sentences below written on a board, a computer, or on pieces of paper, with a choice of two words to fill the gap written separately:
You need to keep your dog _____. clean/dirty
You will only need to _____ your dog every one or two weeks. feed/wash
Make sure the kennel is _____ enough for your dog. big/small
Playing keeps dogs _____. happy/sad

- Ask the children to read the sentences and work out which word should go in the space to make the sentences right.
- Encourage them to use the book, if necessary. Encourage early finishers to find the sentence in the book. Praise the children who re-read the sentence to check if it makes sense.

Word level work

Objective To learn the common spelling patterns for the long vowel phoneme "ee" (W1)

- Read the contents page with the children and ask them to point out any words with the long "ee" vowel sound.
- Ask the children to read through the text and collect other examples, and to group them according to the different spelling patterns.

Speaking and listening activities for groups

Objectives   1d) focus on the main point; 2d) listen to others' reactions; 3a) take turns in speaking; 3e) give reasons for opinions

- Discuss with the children any pets they have, and how they look after them.
- Ask the children to work with a partner, choose a pet and talk about the things they should do to look after it.
- Choose some of the children to tell the rest of the class how to look after a specific pet.

Cross-curricular links
◀▶ **Design and Technology (QCA 1D)**
Plan and design a dog house
PSHE (non-statutory guidelines 2E)
How people and other living things have needs and that they have responsibilities to meet them

Writing

Objective   To use the language and features of non-fiction texts to make class books (T21)

- Read the chapter of instructions about feeding your dog with the children. Discuss how the instructions include a list of what is needed, followed by the steps to be taken.
- Using suggestions from the children, model how to write instructions for feeding a different pet. Scribe some of the children's ideas as part of the model.
- Ask the children to choose another pet, and write a set of instructions for feeding it. Tell them to use appropriate headings, and a numbered list of steps. Collect their pages to make a class book about feeding pets.

Public Art

Reading the book with individuals or guided reading groups

NB for additional and more detailed guidance on guided reading see Stage 5 Guided Reading Cards (available separately, ISBN 0 19 919770 9). Take-Home Cards are also available, providing guidance for parents/carers (ISBN 0 19 919769 5).

Introducing the book

- Look at the front cover. Ask the children what they think this book will be about? Encourage them to look for clues by predicting from the cover illustration.
- Ask the children to read the title and the back cover blurb to confirm their ideas
- Read the contents page together.

During reading

- Encourage the children to read the book. Encourage them to break longer, difficult words into syllables to help them work them out. Don't allow children to struggle for too long when they have difficulty in case they lose the sense of the text.
- Prompt the children to use the picture clues and initial sounds where appropriate.

Observing Check that the children:

- use a variety of strategies to work out new words (T2)
- re-read sentences and use the grammar to predict words (S2)
- read the familiar high frequency words on sight (W2)

After reading

- Ask the children:
  What sort of art is this book about?
  How does the index help you find out information in this book?

Group and independent reading activities

Text level work

Objective To read with sufficient concentration to complete a text, and to identify preferences and give reasons (T4)

- Ask the children to read the text and study the illustrations.
- Tell them to work with a partner and tell each other which piece of public art they prefer.
- Ask them each to write a sentence to say why they prefer their chosen piece of art.
- Have a class vote on which piece they like best, and choose some of the children to read their sentences to the rest of the class.

Sentence level work

Objective Other common uses of capitalization, e.g. for personal titles, headings, book titles, emphasis (S5)

Prepare:
The sentences from the book below written on a board, a computer, or on pieces of paper, using lower case letters:
this fountain is in London.
it is in new Zealand.
these sculptures are in the usa.
it is open from january until march.

- Discuss when capital letters are needed in sentences, i.e. the beginning of a sentence, for names, and using initials for abbreviation
- Ask the children to rewrite the information, adding capital letters in the appropriate places.

Word level work

Objective The common spelling patterns for the long vowel phoneme "ie" (W1)

- Look at the words "Lights" and "Ice" on the contents page with the children.
- Ask them to look through the text and find any other words with the long vowel sound "ie" with the spelling pattern "igh".
- Ask them to find any other ways the sound can be spelt in the text.

Speaking and listening activities for groups

Objective 1d) focus on the main point; 2d) listen to others' reactions; 3a) take turns in speaking; 3e) give reasons for opinions

- Discuss the concept of Public Art with the children. Ask them to work with a partner and think of somewhere in their own environment that could be improved by art.
- Ask some of the children to share their ideas with the class.

Cross-curricular links
◀▶ **Art (QCA 1C)**
What is sculpture?
Art (QCA 2C)
Can buildings speak?
Geography (QCA 1)
AAround our school – the local area

Writing

Objective To write own questions prior to reading for information and to record answers (T22)

- Read the table of contents with the children and ask them to talk about what sort of information they expect to find for each heading.
- Ask them to work with a partner and write a question for three of the headings, using "What", "How" and "Where" to begin their questions.
- Tell the children to swap their questions with their partner, and to use the text to find the answers.
- Ask the children to write their answers underneath the questions.

Wonders of the World

Reading the book with individuals or guided reading groups

NB for additional and more detailed guidance on guided reading see Stage 5 Guided Reading Cards (available separately, ISBN 0 19 919770 9). Take-Home Cards are also available, providing guidance for parents/carers (ISBN 0 19 919769 5).

Introducing the book

- Look at the front cover. Ask the children what type of book this is going to be and encourage them to look for clues, e.g. non-fiction because different photos of the Earth are used.
- Ask the children to find the title and read it together.
- Look at the title page and talk about the illustration.
- Ask the children to read the back cover blurb to confirm their ideas.
- Look through the book and focus on the photographs. Ask the children to say what the photos show. Encourage the children to read the labels on the maps.

During reading

- Encourage the children to read the book. Praise the children when they attempt new words by leaving a gap and predicting words that make sense, e.g. "breathe" on page 3.
- Prompt the children to use their knowledge of sounds and spelling patterns to work out the new and unfamiliar words.

Observing Check that the children:

- use the terms "fiction", "non-fiction", "photograph", and "label" when discussing the book (T17)
- recognize capital letters and full stops (S4)
- recognize common spelling patterns in words (W7)

After reading

- Ask the children:
  How do the photos help you understand the information?
  What do the labels on the maps tell you?

Group and independent reading activities

Text level work

Objective To read non-fiction books and understand that the reader doesn't need to go from start to finish but selects according to what is needed (T18)

- Ask the children:
  Can you show me the page that tells us where the deepest place in the world is? Where is the largest river in the world?
- Tell the children to ask similar questions to a partner, and to scan the text to find the answers.

Sentence level work

Objective To read familiar texts aloud and with pace and expression (S3)

- Ask the children to work with a partner. Tell them to take turns to read each of the sentences on 4 pages of their choice.
- Encourage the children to read with fluency and expression, pausing slightly at full stops, and changing tone when reading the "fact box" information.

Word level work

Objective To learn the common spelling patterns for long vowel phonemes "ee", "ie", and "oa" (W1)

- Read pages 10 and 11 with the children, asking them to point out words with the long vowel sounds, "ee", "ie" and "oa" as you read them.
- Write the words the children find on the board and talk about other ways of spelling the same sound.
- Ask the children to read through the book and to collect words with the same vowel sounds and write them in three columns.

Speaking and listening activities for groups

Objectives 1d) focus on the main point; 2d) listen to others' reactions; 3a) take turns in speaking; 3e) give reasons for opinions

- Discuss with the children what features mean these can be classed as "Wonders of the World".
- Ask the children to think about what they see around them in their own local area.
- Ask them to talk in pairs and together choose something in the local area that could be a "Wonder of Our Area".
- Ask each pair to tell the rest of the class what their choice is, and give a reason for choosing it.

Cross-curricular links
◀▶ **ICT (QCA 1D)**
Labelling and classifying – use personal descriptions to describe objects
Geography
Knowledge and understanding of places

Writing

Objectives To write own questions prior to reading for information and to record answers (T22)

- Discuss how questions can be worded.
- Draw up a list of question words with the children (where, what, how, why).
- Ask them to each write three questions based on the information in the text, and to swap them with a partner, then write the answers to their partner's questions.

Links to other Oxford Reading Tree titles

Fireflies Stage 5	Oxford Reading Tree stories with similar subjects/themes
Magic Tricks	Hey Presto!, A Good Trick, The Play, The Magic Key
Houses	House for Sale, The New House, The Secret Room, A New Classroom,
E-Mails Home	On the Sand, Lucky the Goat, The Dragon Dance, Chinese Adventure
Looking after your Dog	Come In!, Pip at the Zoo, Roy and the Budgie, Noah's Ark Adventure
Public Art	The Lost Key, The Rainbow Machine, The Evil Genie, Save Floppy! William and the Dog
Wonders of the World	The Scarf, Underground Adventure

OXFORD
UNIVERSITY PRESS

Great Clarendon Street, Oxford OX2 6DP

Oxford University Press is a department of the University of Oxford.
It furthers the University's objective of excellence in research,
scholarship, and education by publishing worldwide in

Oxford New York

Auckland Bangkok Buenos Aires Cape Town Chennai
Dar es Salaam Delhi Hong Kong Istanbul Karachi Kolkata Kuala
Lumpur Madrid Melbourne Mexico City Mumbai Nairobi São
Paulo Shanghai Taipei Tokyo Toronto

Oxford is a registered trade mark of Oxford University Press
in the UK and in certain other countries

© Oxford University Press 2003

The moral rights of the author have been asserted

Database right Oxford University Press (maker)

First published 2003

British Library Cataloguing in Publication Data

Data available

Teacher's Notes: ISBN 0 19 919768 7

10 9 8 7 6 5 4 3 2 1

Page make-up by IFA Design Ltd, Plymouth, Devon

Printed in China through Colorcraft Ltd., Hong Kong